LEARNING TO MEDITATE

Concentration & Analytical Meditation

| JUNIPER BOOKS |

Juniper Books is an imprint of Juniper Foundation,
a 501(c)(3) non-profit organization.

www.juniperpath.org

The purpose of a spiritual path is to take us beyond inner dogmas and habitual patterns of thinking and behavior in order to deeply develop conscious experience. Otherwise, conditioned concepts of who we are—as a result of our upbringing, education, communities, culture, and so on—lock us into ways of being that can bring stress, hardship, and confusion, and most importantly, that can block the fruition of our inner potential.

Cofounded by Buddhist master Segyu Rinpoche and four longtime students, Juniper is extending into modern culture a profound Buddhist lineage for developing the mind. By extracting the essence of Buddhist thought from the cultural wrapper in which we receive it, Juniper is making the path of Buddhist training relevant and accessible. This rich methodology and way of being has much to offer in contemporary life, and Juniper's aim is to open the door for those seeking to embrace it.

Learning to Meditate provides instruction on how to begin and develop a meditation practice. It is suitable for beginners, and for experienced meditators seeking to learn meditation in this tradition.

What Is Meditation?

*The best way to develop the mind is
through gradual change and refinement,
like dripping water that slowly smoothes
jagged rock. Meditation is the water,
gradually refining and polishing the
mind.*

Meditation is the foundation of training the mind. It comprises a rich collection of practices that cultivate focus, stability, insight, and awareness. We can think of meditation as exercise for the mind. Just as physical exercise strengthens the body, meditation strengthens the mind. Similarly, just as reading about the benefits of physical exercise will not make us physically fit, intellectual knowledge about meditation will not make us inwardly fit. Meditating, and putting what we gain in meditation to work, is the springboard for our inner journey.

We define meditation as the act of concentrating on an object that enhances the mind. "Concentrating" describes the act of focusing the mind and bringing inner distraction and agitation under control. "On an object" means that meditation is not about turning our minds off or spacing out but is about anchoring the mind on a particular object and keeping it there. "Enhances the mind" means that in meditation we do not pick just any object but use objects that enhance our strength of mind and free our inner potential. These objects include the breath, visualized images, or insights gained from reflecting upon specific topics or ideas.

Meditation is a space that we carve out each day to turn inward. It is important to follow meditation instructions that are clear and precise, but we do not have to be too rigid. We can develop a way of practicing that suits our own lifestyle and schedule. The length, frequency, and objects of meditation, for example, might vary from one person to another and will evolve as we gain experience.

At Juniper we practice two principle types of meditation: concentration meditation and analytical meditation. In concentration meditation, we hold the mind on an object, such as the breath or a visualized image, in order to strengthen our focus and to cultivate peacefulness by overcoming inner agitation and lethargy. In analytical meditation, we focus the mind on specific topics, applying our capacity for contemplation and reason to raise our awareness so that these ideas take hold within us at a deep level. Both of these meditations use the same basic structure, which we will present in the next section.

Often, when we first try meditation of any kind, we encounter the mind's state of agitation head-on. After just a few seconds the mind wanders. We bring it back and it wanders again. Over and over it drifts, jumping from one thought to another. Or we may find ourselves drowsy or falling asleep, unable to concentrate on anything at all. The mind oscillates between excitement and lethargy, like a little dog that is either barking excitedly or sleeping. As we work on meditation, however, we develop more capacity to bring these inner swings under control and to make the mind more stable and serene. Eventually, we find that this healthier state of mind is not something we experience only during meditation; it will begin to influence all our endeavors, bringing to everything we do a more patient, calm, and serene inner state.

Meditation is a learned skill, something in which we build competence over time. Proficiency in meditation is acquired through repeated effort. The best way to develop the mind is through gradual change and refinement, like dripping water that slowly smoothes jagged rock. Meditation is the water, gradually refining and polishing the mind. Therefore, regular practice is more important than the length of the practice; it is better to have a meditation session for even a few minutes daily than to have longer sessions less frequently.

The basic structure of meditation has three aspects:

- Preparation
- Setting the object
- Bringing the mind back

In the next session, we will cover these three aspects while describing how to do concentration meditation.

Concentration Meditation

We recommend meditating in short sessions, such as five minutes, especially at the outset. Making a habit of meditation will help build the capacity to stay focused on the object.

Concentration meditation is the foundation of one's meditation practice. In concentration meditation, we hold the mind on an object, such as the breath or a visualized image, in order to strengthen our focus and to cultivate peacefulness by overcoming inner agitation and lethargy. We develop this practice by following the three aspects of meditation: preparation, setting the object, and bringing the mind back.

Preparation

When we do physical exercise, we are accustomed to making preparations. We must decide when to exercise (morning, lunchtime, evening, or weekends), make sure we are physically ready (wear the right clothes and ensure the stomach is not too full), and decide where to exercise (home, gym, or outdoors). Meditation is similar in that we need to take some simple steps to prepare. It is better to think of the preparation as part of the meditation itself, because the process of preparation helps us to calm down and turn inward. Preparing to meditate has three elements: time, place, and posture.

TIME

It is best to pick a set time to meditate, beginning with at least five minutes and extending the time as the habit of meditation becomes more stable. Possibilities include when we wake up, after breakfast, before dinner, before we go to bed, or any other convenient time. The time of day itself does not matter as much as our commitment to it. We can, of course, change the time or alter it according to our schedule, but it is good to have in mind a set time. It is also good to make it a daily endeavor. Five minutes a day is better than an hour on the weekends. It is fine if we miss a day here and there but we recommend a commitment to a daily meditation practice at a particular time. If you wish, it is often helpful to use a countdown timer to set a specific time period for your meditation session.

PLACE

Surprisingly, it can be challenging to find a good place to meditate. The difficulty of finding a clean, quiet place to sit for a short time is perhaps testimony to the amount of distraction in our lives and the need to meditate. It is not easy to remove ourselves from phones, computers, TV, and other distractions, so we need to put a little effort into it. We recommend picking one place to meditate and sticking to it—any clean and reasonably quiet place where you can sit for a little while undisturbed. Of course, if you are traveling, then you could find any place that works while you are away (the beach or the mountains, for example, can be wonderful places to meditate).

POSTURE

It is important to pay attention to our posture when we meditate. This has a dual effect. First, we can meditate more comfortably and for longer periods when we have good posture. Second, keeping the body in a good posture helps our inner energy and vitality to flow better. Because we are all physically different, there is no formula for how to sit correctly during meditation. We have to experiment until we find what works. Consider this effort part of the meditation itself. As we grow accustomed to meditation, it is likely that our posture will evolve. There are several aspects of meditation posture to consider.

- *Floor or chair:* We recommend sitting upright on the floor or in a chair. We do not recommend lying down because it is too easy to fall asleep. If your legs can handle it, we suggest trying to sit on the floor; otherwise, a chair is fine.
- *Legs:* If you are on the floor, you can cross your legs in the lotus, half-lotus, or ordinary cross-legged position. Any comfortable cross-legged position will work as long as you can sustain it for a little while. Because we are unaccustomed to sitting cross-legged, we generally need one or more cushions to sit on, and sometimes a small cushion under each knee. The goal is to raise the hips and buttocks so the knees rest firmly on the floor. Any reasonably firm cushions will do.
- *Spine and shoulders:* Try to keep the spine erect. If it slouches as you meditate, straighten it again. Keep the shoulders relaxed, not tight or hunched up.
- *Eyes:* It is best not to have the eyes fully open, because there are too many distractions, nor fully closed, because this makes it easier to fall asleep. If you can, close the eyes almost all the way, allowing in just a sliver of light.

- *Hands:* We recommend placing the hands in your lap, palms up, with the right palm resting gently in the left, and the ends of the thumbs gently touching.

It is best not to be too rigid in finding the right posture. You can have a great meditation without twisting the legs into uncomfortable positions. Experiment to see what works.

Setting the object

The second aspect of meditation is setting the object. In meditation we do not "space out" or allow the mind to drift. It always involves focusing the mind on an object that has the capacity to enhance and strengthen the mind. In concentration meditation, we want to anchor the mind on the object, and keep it there, so it is important to decide ahead of time what the object of our meditation will be. As we will see later, in analytical meditation we apply reflection and reason on particular topics in order to establish the object of meditation.

There are many possible objects for concentration meditation, including physical objects such as the breath or visualized objects such as a small blue orb of light at the center of the chest (heart center) or a small Buddha Shakyamuni or Buddha Tara image in front of us. We recommend beginning with the breath and adding additional objects later.

To set the object, in the case of the breath, we have to decide exactly how and where we will focus on the breath. Our recommendation is to breathe normally and naturally. Then pick one spot where you feel the breath. One possibility is the abdomen, where the belly moves in and out. Another possibility is the tips of the nostrils, where you can feel the breath coming in and out. The important point is to make a clear commitment to that location. At the beginning of your meditation, take a breath or two to relax, then focus the mind on your object of meditation. Bring your attention to it and try to keep it there.

Bringing the mind back

The third aspect of meditation is bringing the mind back. After we start to meditate, it will not take long for the mind to wander. Maybe a few seconds. This is normal. The mind is active, and the first thing meditation does is remind us of that. Observe the distraction, trying not to become wrapped up in it, and gently bring your attention back to the object of meditation—in this case, the breath.

For a great many individuals, this is easier said than done. It is as if our minds have minds of their own. We want to focus the mind in one direction but it is going headlong in another. Our minds may be excited and distracted, focusing on the issues or emotions of the day, or our minds may be lethargic, taking the opportunity to drift off sleepily. This is all normal. This is one reason we recommend meditating in short sessions, such as five or ten minutes, especially at the outset. Making a habit of meditation will help build the capacity to stay focused on the object. Just bring the mind back to the breath as well as you can.

Sometimes it helps to count the breath as you focus on it. This provides an additional anchor. Counting each in-and-out breath as one, count down from twenty to one, repeating the cycle when you are finished. If your mind drifts from focusing on your breath before you make it all the way down to one, start again from twenty.

These, then, are the three aspects of meditation: preparation, setting the object and bringing the mind back. As your practice develops you can expand it in a number of ways. For example, you can lengthen the time of your meditation session, count down from a higher number, or not count at all and just focus on the breath. You can also add other objects of meditation, such as the visualized images described earlier.

Analytical Meditation

Instead of accepting ideas without question, Buddhist training encourages us to reflect and apply critical thought to test their validity. This generates the grounds on which we can refute the thoughts and inner patterns that create hardship and enhance those that bring insight and well-being.

We have now covered concentration meditation, which is the foundation of one's meditation practice. In analytical meditation we use the mind's capacity for critical thought to examine specific topics that will enhance our awareness and help us grow. For example, these include the topics covered in Juniper's *Awakening the Mind*, such as balancing emotions, compassion, and insight, each broken down into elements suitable for meditation. By bringing the mind to reflect and reason on these topics, we gain the capacity to critically evaluate and refute the inner stories and patterns of behavior that cause us hardship, and to enhance the positive qualities and potential that are more latent within us.

In analytical meditation, the first step, Preparation, is the same as in concentration meditation, whereby we pay attention to time, place and posture in the same way. Then, instead of setting the mind on an object such as the breath, we engage in the following four steps to establish our object of meditation:

- Familiarity
- Reason
- Application
- Insight

1. Familiarity

Familiarity is the process of learning, understanding, or deepening our knowledge of a topic. Buddhist training is based on a rich source of ideas about life, the mind, and experience. Some of these ideas are directed at enhancing our awareness of who we are and how we behave in the world. Others are directed at deepening our insight into the nature of reality and the world around us. Still others are focused on our relationships with and actions toward others. Applied correctly, these topics can have a profound effect on our state of mind and inner well-being.

One of the functions of analytical meditation is to help us become familiar with topics that can enhance experience, bringing them to mind and making sure that we understand them. As the first part of analytical meditation, this can take the form of reading a text or notes, or recalling a discussion, and mentally reviewing them.

To illustrate, let us see how we might apply Familiarity to the following passage from *Awakening the Mind*:

> "Our outer endeavors, such as relationships, jobs, material gains, recreation and so on, may serve different purposes and fulfill us in various ways, but they often do little to address our inner state. On the contrary, our inner state frequently sets

the mood and tone for how we experience outer endeavors."

When using analytical meditation to enhance our familiarity with this passage, during our meditation we might read the passage one or more times and make sure we comprehend what it is saying, recalling perhaps a lesson or other reading we have heard or done on the topic. Thus, Familiarity in analytical meditation means reviewing the content and making sure we understand it.

2. Reason

The next part of analytical meditation is the application of reason and critical thinking to see if what we are examining makes sense. Instead of accepting ideas without question, Buddhist training encourages us to reflect and apply critical thought to test their validity. This generates the grounds on which we can refute the thoughts and inner patterns that create hardship and enhance those that bring insight and well-being.

In applying reason to a topic during meditation, we might ask questions such as:

- Does the idea make sense?
- On what basis might I consider it correct: logic, science, the testimony of others whom I trust, etc.?
- Does it ring true with my experience?
- Are there counterarguments that contradict this idea?

By working with the material in this way, we will exercise our faculty of critical thought, and our capacity for this type of inquiry will grow.

When engaging this part of the meditation, it is important to recognize the difference between critical thought and judgment. The goal is not to judge the material as good or bad, or right or wrong, but to consider it as objectively as we can.

Here is how we might apply reasoning to the earlier passage from *Awakening the Mind*:

> *"Our outer endeavors, such as relationships, jobs, material gains, recreation and so on, may serve different purposes and fulfill us in various ways, but they often do little to address our inner state. On the contrary, our inner state frequently sets the mood and tone for how we experience outer endeavors."*

To apply reason to this statement, we might ask:

- Does it make sense that outer endeavors, such as our jobs, relationships and leisure activities, rarely result in changes to our inner state? Is it more accurate that our inner state will influence how we experience outer endeavors?
- In my experience, do one's activities bring about inner changes?
- How much does our inner feeling influence the mood and tone of our experience? Do I notice how the experience of the exact same activity can change depending on how I feel inwardly?

The purpose of this effort is not so much to reach the right answer as it is to work with the content and stir our minds to thinking about it. The process itself will increase our awareness and open our minds to new possibilities and ideas.

3. Application

Up to this point, we have been examining a topic objectively, making sure we understand it and seeing if it makes sense. The next step is to examine how we might apply the topic to modify our experience right now by diminishing harmful thoughts and actions and enhancing positive thoughts and actions. For example, we might ask:

- Does this apply to me?
- Is there something here to which I should pay attention?
- Does this give me ideas about how to approach situations differently?

Again, let us apply this to the sample topic we have been considering:

> *"Our outer endeavors, such as relationships, jobs, material gains, recreation and so on, may serve different purposes and fulfill us in various ways, but they often do little to address our inner state. On the contrary, our inner state frequently sets the mood and tone for how we experience outer endeavors."*

Here is how we might consider the application of this topic in our own lives:

- How well do my outer endeavors, such as jobs, relationships, material gains and recreation, enhance my inner state? Do they change me in lasting and positive ways?
- How much does my inner state influence my experience in these outer endeavors? What is it that my mood and emotions bring to the situation?
- Can I tell how much of my stress or anxiety is created by my own reactions rather than by the situation itself?

Examining how the topic might apply in our own lives takes it from the theoretical to the pragmatic, and helps us see how the topic might apply directly in our lives right now.

4. Insight

The final aspect of analytical meditation is to deepen any insight that may arise from the topic we are examining by making it our object of concentration. As we progress in analytical meditation, we will invariably have instances of clarity, when something clicks—an "Aha!" moment. Examples might include:

- "Now I know what this is saying; finally, I get it."
- "I never saw myself that way before."
- "Now I see how to be different in that situation. I know what to do."
- "I handled that better than before; I'm proud of myself."

There are many types of insights we might gain, each characterized by an "I get it!" feeling. This may not happen all the time, but when it does we want to solidify it. This is the part of the analytical meditation where we do that.

In the Insight aspect of analytical meditation, the goal is to focus on any insight we may have had. We make this insight the object of concentration, and we focus the mind on it for a little while.

Applying this to our example might look like this:

> "Our outer endeavors, such as relationships, jobs, material gains, recreation and so on, may serve different purposes and fulfill us in various ways, but they often do little to address our inner state. On the contrary, our inner state frequently sets the mood and tone for how we experience outer endeavors."

Here are some possible insights we might gain after contemplating this:

- "Now I see how I am investing in endeavors that are not all that fulfilling."
- "Now I see how my own actions and behavior are impeding my relationships."
- "Now I see why I should pay attention to my inner patterns."

In this part of the meditation, we rest the mind on any insight, concentrating on it for a while, as if giving it the chance to take root within us. We will find that, as we develop experience with meditation, the quality and depth of the insights we gain, and their application in our lives, will evolve.

Familiarity, Reason, Application and Insight are the four stages of analytical meditation. We can apply them to each line or paragraph of Awakening the Mind, using them to discover and probe the meaning of the ideas presented and to see how they apply in our lives. We also recommend attending a Juniper class or retreat in order to learn the various topics of analytical meditation from a teacher with experience in these methods. As our own experience grows, our capacity for analytical meditation will increase and soon we will have in our hands a rich tool for enhancing our awareness, deepening our understanding, and furthering our spiritual growth.

A Healthy Approach

*Meditation should be a respite from the
pressures of performance. Go easy on
yourself. Be happy that you are making
space to meditate.*

As you develop your meditation practice, following a few basic
guidelines will help to cultivate a healthy approach that enhances
your progress:

- Be patient
- Don't compare
- Enjoy simplicity
- Make it a habit
- Relax

Be patient

Proficiency in meditation is a gradual process, so if we are looking
for immediate results we might become frustrated. We mentioned
earlier how meditation works like water dripping onto a jagged rock.
We may not see the effect of each drop, but over time the rock
becomes smooth and beautiful. Think of each moment of effort—
preparation, setting the object, bringing the mind back—as one
drop. Results will come from accumulating a steady stream of

drops, so when it comes to meditation it is best to cultivate an attitude of steadiness and patience.

Don't compare

Meditation is not about performance. It is about you and your mind. We all start at different places and we all progress in different ways. We can easily be fooled by one person who looks like a great meditator, another who eloquently articulates nuances of Buddhist philosophy, or another who can barely do either. These are merely outer signs that tell us little about one's inner state. Thus, it can be very misleading to judge or compare oneself with others. Meditation is a time to turn off the inner pressures that say you have to be one thing or another. You may feel that your meditation is progressing slowly or not at all, or you may find some meditation days are better than others, but important inner changes still may be taking place.

Enjoy simplicity

Do not be in a hurry to make your meditation practice longer or more complicated. There are many types of meditation, some simple and some involving extensive visualizations. It is tempting to think that the more complex your meditation, the more advanced your practice. However, this is a false assumption. Sometimes the simplest meditations can be the most potent, and one's capacity to do more complex meditations may not be a reflection of inner growth or development but simply a reflection of the desire to achieve. We recommend sticking with the simple for a while. Even when you do extend your practice, come back to the simple every now and again.

Make it a habit

The best way to see results is by making your meditation a habit. We recommend a daily meditation practice, for five minutes or longer. If you aim for a daily practice, there is a higher chance that meditation will become a healthy habit in your life. By having a daily practice, you will tend to engage in a regular practice even if you miss a day here and there.

Relax

Above all, relax. In our attainment-oriented culture, meditation should be a respite from the pressures of performance. Go easy on yourself. Be happy that you are making space to meditate. Enjoy the connection with a spiritual lineage of masters and adepts. Allow their efforts and these teachings to energize you. Try to stay content and relaxed as you embark on this journey.

Developing a Practice

*Meditation is a methodology to release
the mind from the thoughts, emotions
and actions that bring us hardship and to
give us the awareness that brings peace,
joy, insight and vitality to everything we
do.*

A meditation practice is meant to be a rich and important part of
one's life. It is a time each day to turn inward and cultivate the
quality of mind that will enhance all aspects of our lives. Whether
we meditate first thing in the morning, at night before we go to bed,
or any other time, a meditation practice assures that, each day, we
spend some time away from the distractions and noise of our lives,
and nourish ourselves inwardly.

There is no single formula for building a meditation practice. It
is best when it fits into the rhythm of our lives, and it will almost
certainly evolve and change as our experience and circumstances
change. However, following a few guidelines will help us gain the
most from our meditation practice. These are:

- Concentration meditation as the foundation
- Study with a school or teacher
- Watch your mind between sessions

Concentration meditation as the foundation

In general, concentration meditation should be the foundation of one's practice. For some individuals, analytical meditation might be a little easier because we are already familiar with what it means to contemplate a topic, whereas concentration meditation disciplines the mind in a less familiar way. Nevertheless, it is important to build up the practice of holding the mind on an object so we recommend that, for at least five minutes a day, use concentration meditation as the foundation of your practice.

It is fine to begin with concentration meditation alone. It is more important to develop the habit of meditation than to overly complicate one's practice. Therefore, add the analytical meditation as and when you feel ready.

Study with a school or teacher

Although we can easily learn the technique of meditation from a book, meditation is not intended as a self-help methodology. Whenever possible, it is best to study with a school or teacher who can answer questions, provide guidance, refine our practice, and so on. Therefore, an essential part of developing a meditation practice is to consult with a teacher or attend classes, retreats or workshops in the school of practice you are following.

Watch your mind between sessions

It is often said that the most important meditation is the meditation we do between the times we actually sit and meditate. Meditation is a methodology to release the mind from the thoughts, emotions and actions that bring us hardship and to give us the awareness that brings peace, joy, insight and vitality to everything we do. It is a means to grow and enhance our potential. This calls for paying attention to our minds throughout the day, not just when we are sitting in meditation.

Summary

Concentration Meditation

PREPARATION

Time. Commit to a fixed daily time to meditate. If you wish, use a countdown timer to set a specific time period for your meditation session. Begin with at least five minutes and build up as your meditation becomes stable.

Place. Commit to one place to meditate that is quiet and where you will be uninterrupted.

Posture. Either sit cross-legged on the floor, with cushions for support, or sit in a chair. Keep your spine erect, shoulders relaxed, and hands in your lap, palms up, with the right hand resting on the left and thumbs touching. Close your eyes almost all the way, allowing in a sliver of light.

SETTING THE OBJECT

Select an object of meditation, beginning with your breath. Breathe naturally and focus on the flow of your breath in the abdomen or at the tips of the nostrils.

BRINGING THE MIND BACK

As your mind wanders, gently bring it back to restore your focus on the object. If you wish, count down from twenty to one, counting each in-and-out breath as one. Start again when you are finished or if your mind drifts from your breath. When the time is up, take a deep breath and bring the session to an end.

Analytical Meditation

FAMILIARITY
Review a topic to become familiar with its ideas and understand it.

REASON
Review a topic to see if it makes sense according to logic, science, the testimony of others or your own experience.

APPLICATION
Review a topic to see how it applies in your life: How is it relevant to your own experiences and state of mind?

INSIGHT
Keep the mind focused on any insight arising from the previous steps—an "Aha!" moment—and make the insight the object of concentration meditation.

A Healthy Approach

- Be patient
- Don't compare
- Enjoy simplicity
- Make it a habit
- Relax

Developing a Practice

- Concentration meditation as the foundation
- Study with a school or teacher
- Watch your mind between sessions

For more information about Juniper's programs and work, please visit www.juniperpath.org or contact Juniper at team@juniperpath.org.